PAUL REVERE DIDN'T SAY "THE BRITISH ARE COMING!"

EXPOSING MYTHS ABOUT THE AMERICAN REVOLUTION

BY SHALINI SAXENA

 Gareth Stevens
PUBLISHING

Please visit our website, www.garethstevens.com. For a free color catalog of all our high-quality books, call toll free 1-800-542-2595 or fax 1-877-542-2596.

Library of Congress Cataloging-in-Publication Data

Names: Saxena, Shalini, 1982- author.
Title: Paul Revere didn't say "The British are coming!" : exposing myths about the American Revolution / Shalini Saxena.
Description: New York : Gareth Stevens Publishing, 2017. | Series: Exposed! Myths about early American history | Includes index.
Identifiers: LCCN 2016037196| ISBN 9781482457278 (pbk. book) | ISBN 9781482457285 (6 pack) | ISBN 9781482457292 (library bound book)
Subjects: LCSH: United States–History–Revolution, 1775-1783–Juvenile literature. | United States–History–Errors, inventions, etc.–Juvenile literature.
Classification: LCC E208 .S294 2017 | DDC 973.3–dc23
LC record available at https://lccn.loc.gov/2016037196

First Edition

Published in 2017 by
Gareth Stevens Publishing
111 East 14th Street, Suite 349
New York, NY 10003

Copyright © 2017 Gareth Stevens Publishing

Designer: Sarah Liddell
Editor: Therese Shea

Photo credits: Cover, p. 1 Ed Vebell/Contributor/Archive Photos/Getty Images; background texture used throughout IS MODE/Shutterstock.com; ripped newspaper used throughout STILLFX/Shutterstock.com; photo corners used throughout Carolyn Franks/Shutterstock.com; p. 5, 11 (Longfellow) Library of Congress/Contributor/Corbis Historical/Getty Images; p. 7 DEA PICTURE LIBRARY/Contributor/De Agostini/Getty Images; p. 9 Cropbot/Wikimedia Commons; pp. 11 (poem), 15 Midnightdreary/Wikimedia Commons; p. 13 Hulton Archive/Stringer/Hulton Archive/Getty Images; p. 14 Christian Delbert/Shutterstock.com; p. 17 Francis G. Mayer/Corbis Historical/Getty Images; p. 19 Interim Archives/Contributor/Archive Photos/Getty Images; p. 21 (main) Scewing/Wikimedia Commons; p. 21 (Treaty of Paris) Flickr upload bot/Wikimedia Commons; p. 23 Popperfoto/Contributor/Popperfoto/Getty Images; p. 25 Davepape/Wikimedia Commons; p. 27 Hohum/Wikimedia Commons; p. 29 Ken Thomas/Getty Images.

Printed in China

CPSIA compliance information: Batch #CW17GS: For further information contact Gareth Stevens, New York, New York at 1-800-542-2595.

CONTENTS

Words in the glossary appear in **bold** type the first time they are used in the text.

SEPARATING MYTH AND FACT

Every summer, millions of Americans **celebrate** Independence Day. Between picnics and fireworks, they remember that July 4 was an important date in American history. They celebrate the 13 American colonies gaining freedom from British rule. But it might come as a shock to some that the colonists were far from free on July 4, 1776. The American Revolution had begun, but there was still much fighting to come.

Many accounts from the American Revolution mix historical facts and **myths**. Read on to find out what really happened!

5

A DIVIDED POPULATION

MOST COLONISTS WANTED INDEPENDENCE BEFORE THE REVOLUTION STARTED.

THE FACTS:

Since the 1760s, England had established taxes and practices in its colonies that many believed were unfair. It's often thought that most colonists wanted freedom from England when the American Revolution first began in 1775.

Though many colonists were upset, some didn't want independence. They simply wanted a say in decisions made by the British government that would affect them. Colonists put on **protests** such as the Boston Tea Party to show their unhappiness with British laws.

NO TEACUPS HERE

In 1773, England passed a law that hurt the sales of colonial tea merchants. In protest, 60 or so colonists dressed as Native Americans dumped 300 crates, or boxes, of tea into Boston Harbor on December 16, 1773. This event became known as the Boston Tea Party.

After the Boston Tea Party, Boston Harbor was closed to **punish** the colonists. This only made colonists angrier and more willing to break away from England.

THE MIDNIGHT RIDE

PAUL REVERE RODE
ALONE ONE NIGHT SHOUTING,
"THE BRITISH ARE COMING!"

THE FACTS:

On the night of April 18, 1775, American **patriot** Paul
Revere *did* go on a late night ride to tell colonists that
British troops were planning to capture colonial supplies.

However, Revere wasn't alone, and he probably never
shouted because he didn't want British soldiers to hear
him! Also, colonists considered themselves British, too, so
Revere more likely called the British troops "Regulars."

British soldiers captured Paul Revere before he reached Concord, Massachusetts, where he was planning to go. By then, however, he had already warned many colonists, who were able to prepare to face the British.

Myths often have many roots. It can be hard to figure out how they began. With the story of Paul Revere, though, we actually have an idea about its origin. In 1861, American poet Henry Wadsworth Longfellow wrote a poem titled "Paul Revere's Ride." The work got some facts wrong, but it became famous, spreading Revere's story.

According to Longfellow, Revere rode alone and reached Concord. But Revere was actually joined by fellow patriots William Dawes and Samuel Prescott. In fact, Prescott was the only rider to make it to Concord!

A MAN OF MANY HATS

In addition to being a patriot, Paul Revere was a silversmith, a kind of dentist, and a spy! In fact, he belonged to a group of colonial spies called the "Mechanics."

Longfellow wrote "Paul Revere's Ride" nearly 100 years after it actually took place.

LONGFELLOW'S POEM

PAUL REVERE'S RIDE.

LISTEN, my children, and you shall hear
Of the midnight ride of Paul Revere,
On the eighteenth of April, in Seventy-Five:
Hardly a man is now alive
Who remembers that famous day and year.

He said to his friend, — " If the British march
By land or sea from the town to-night,
Hang a lantern aloft in the belfry-arch
Of the North-Church-tower, as a signal-light, —
One if by land, and two if by sea;
And I on the opposite shore will be,
Ready to ride and spread the alarm
Through every Middlesex village and farm,
For the country-folk to be up and to arm."

Then he said good-night, and with muffled oar
Silently rowed to the Charlestown shore,
Just as the moon rose over the bay,
Where swinging wide at her moorings lay
The Somerset, British man-of-war :
A phantom ship, with each mast and spar
Across the moon, like a prison-bar,
And a huge, black hulk, that was magnified
By its own reflection in the tide.

Meanwhile, his friend, through alley and street
Wanders and watches with eager ears,
Till in the silence around him he hears
The muster of men at the barrack-door,
The sound of arms, and the tramp of feet,
And the measured tread of the grenadiers
Marching down to their boats on the shore.

Then he climbed to the tower of the church,
Up the wooden stairs, with stealthy tread,

HENRY WADSWORTH
LONGFELLOW

11

"THE SHOT HEARD 'ROUND THE WORLD"

THE MYTH: THE FIRST SHOT OF THE AMERICAN REVOLUTION WAS FIRED IN CONCORD, MASSACHUSETTS.

THE FACTS:

On April 19, 1775, British troops headed toward the town of Concord to capture and destroy colonial supplies that were stored there. However, they reached nearby Lexington, Massachusetts, first. Thanks to the warnings the night before, the colonists in Lexington were ready for a fight.

It's very likely that this is where the first shot was fired, not in Concord as many believe. However, we still don't know who fired first—the American colonists or the British soldiers.

AT A MINUTE'S NOTICE

Massachusetts leaders called on colonists to form special fighting forces made up of "minutemen." These fighters were ready for battle "at a minute's notice." That's how they got their name!

The Battle of Lexington took place just hours before the Battle of Concord. By the end of the day, the colonists had forced the British back to Boston, Massachusetts.

13

Emerson wrote "Concord Hymn" in honor of the opening of this monument, which stands near the North Bridge where the Battle of Concord took place.

Like the myths about Paul Revere, a writer started the myth of the first shot of the American Revolution. Ralph Waldo Emerson spent much of his life in Concord. In 1837, he wrote a poem called "Concord Hymn" about the famous battle that had happened there.

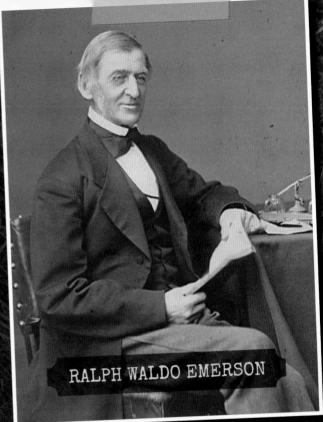

RALPH WALDO EMERSON

He penned the line "the shot heard 'round the world" about the opening of the battle. Over time, many believed it was about the first shot of the war—which had probably occurred at Lexington earlier that day.

THE BATTLE OF BUNKER HILL

THE FIRST MAJOR BATTLE OF THE AMERICAN REVOLUTION WAS FOUGHT ON BUNKER HILL.

THE FACTS:

On the night of June 16, 1775, colonial forces set out to **fortify** Bunker Hill outside of Boston to protect it from the British. For some reason, however, the colonial leader, William Prescott, had the soldiers fortify neighboring Breed's Hill instead.

The fighting began the next morning. Breed's Hill was lower than Bunker Hill and much closer to the British. The British easily fired on colonial troops and charged up the hill, **defeating** the colonists.

Despite taking place on Breed's Hill, the important battle
is known by most as the Battle of Bunker Hill.

NOT A TOTAL LOSS

Although the colonists lost, the
battle actually gave them **confidence**.
Many more British soldiers had been
killed or wounded. American forces
had held their own.

17

THE FACTS:

Israel Putnam served as an American colonel at the Battle of Bunker Hill. He was said to have told his troops not to fire at the British until they could "see the whites of their eyes."

That order was just a popular saying. If the colonists had held their fire until the British were that close, many more Americans would have died. The colonists probably opened fire at about 50 yards (46 m), too far to see anyone's eyes closely.

Israel Putnam is said to have left his farm in the middle of plowing to join the American Revolution.

ISRAEL PUTNAM

19

THE REAL INDEPENDENCE DAY

JULY 4, 1776, WAS THE DAY THE COLONISTS VOTED FOR INDEPENDENCE.

THE FACTS:

July 4, 1776, has long been known as Independence Day in the United States. But the colonies didn't have independence yet. July 4 is still an important date, though—it's the day the **Continental Congress** adopted the **document** called the Declaration of Independence in Philadelphia, Pennsylvania. They had actually voted for independence 2 days before, on July 2, 1776.

People didn't begin celebrating July 4 as a special day until 1777—even though they still weren't free yet!

Thomas Jefferson, along with Benjamin Franklin, Roger Sherman, Robert Livingston, and John Adams, wrote the Declaration of Independence. It officially declares, or states, the independence of the colonies and the reasons they were breaking away from England.

SIGNATURES ON THE TREATY OF PARIS

A NEW HOLIDAY?

The Treaty of Paris was the agreement that officially ended the American Revolution. The document was signed on September 3, 1783.

THE FAMED WATER CARRIER

THE MYTH: MOLLY PITCHER WAS AN AMERICAN SOLDIER'S WIFE WHO OPERATED HER HUSBAND'S CANNON WHEN HE COULD NO LONGER DO IT.

THE FACTS:

Parts of this myth could be true, but there's no proof. Some historians believe a woman named Molly Hays was the real Molly Pitcher. Her husband is known to have served during the Battle of Monmouth in 1778. She carried pitchers, or jugs, of water to him and other soldiers. He's said to have fallen down in battle because of the heat, causing Molly to take his place at a cannon.

Other historians say the story mixes up different women who helped the American cause during the revolution.

22

We may not know if Molly Hays was the real Molly Pitcher, but we do know that she played a part in the American Revolution and was later paid for it.

MOLLY PITCHER

UNSUNG HEROES

Although women weren't allowed to be soldiers, they played major roles in the revolution. For example, Deborah Samson dressed as a man and served in the army, while 16-year-old Sybil Ludington rode many miles to warn colonists of a British attack.

23

LOST CHANCES

THE FACTS:

There were a few chances for the British army to win the war or at least win some important battles. In 1777, British general William Howe could have worked with British general John Burgoyne to take control of the Hudson River. This would have cut New England off from the rest of the colonies.

However, Howe chose to have his forces attack Philadelphia, Pennsylvania, because the Continental Congress was there. Burgoyne's soldiers were then defeated in Saratoga, New York.

THINK FAST

In 1776, General Howe had the colonists' Continental army almost totally surrounded in New York. However, he was slow to act and allowed them to slip away.

In this painting, Burgoyne **surrenders** to Continental army general Horatio Gates (center) at Saratoga on October 17, 1777.

GENERAL WASHINGTON

THE MYTH: GEORGE WASHINGTON'S EXCELLENT BATTLE PLANS WON THE WAR.

THE FACTS:

Many think George Washington, the commander in chief of the Continental army, was the reason the Americans won independence.

However, military historians note that key failures during the American Revolution were due to Washington's slow decision-making. This led to the British taking New York's Fort Washington and New Jersey's Fort Lee in November 1776, for example. In fact, the Americans' French **allies** led the Battle of Yorktown in 1781, which ended the war.

Washington may not have been wholly responsible for America's success in the war, but he **inspired** his soldiers to be brave in hard times, such as the winter of 1777 to 1778 at Valley Forge, Pennsylvania.

AN HONEST MAN

Washington never said he was a great military leader. In fact, he told the Continental Congress in 1776 that he had "limited and contracted knowledge . . . in Military Matters."

27

REMEMBERING THE REVOLUTION

The stories of the revolution, whether true or false, still inspire patriotism throughout the United States. Remembering the people and events of that time helps us remember the struggles the country faced before it became an independent nation.

Thanks to the many who gave their lives, freedom remains an important idea in the United States. Although there's much about the revolution that may have been lost to history or turned to myth, there's also much we should never forget.

This monument in Philadelphia, Pennsylvania, honors those who died in the American Revolution.

FREEDOM IS A LIGHT
FOR WHICH MANY MEN HAVE DIED IN DARKNESS

IN UNMARKED GRAVES WITHIN
THIS SQUARE LIE THOUSANDS
OF UNKNOWN SOLDIERS OF
WASHINGTON'S ARMY WHO DIED
OF WOUNDS AND SICKNESS DURING
THE REVOLUTIONARY WAR

THE INDEPENDENCE AND LIBERTY
YOU POSSESS ARE THE WORK OF
JOINT COUNCILS AND JOINT
EFFORTS-OF COMMON DANGERS,
SUFFERINGS AND SUCCESS.
WASHINGTON'S FAREWELL ADDRESS SEPT. 17, 1796

AN AMERICAN REVOLUTION TIMELINE

1773
COLONISTS TAKE PART IN THE
BOSTON TEA PARTY.

1775
THE BRITISH DEFEAT THE
AMERICANS AT THE BATTLE OF
BUNKER HILL ON JUNE 17.

1777–1778
AMERICAN FORCES BRAVE
HARD CONDITIONS DURING A
WINTER AT VALLEY FORGE.

1781
THE BRITISH ARMY
SURRENDERS AT YORKTOWN,
VIRGINIA, ON OCTOBER 19.

1775
PAUL REVERE MAKES HIS
FAMOUS RIDE ON APRIL 18.

1775
THE BATTLES OF LEXINGTON AND
CONCORD TAKE PLACE ON APRIL 19.

1777
THE BRITISH ARE DEFEATED
IN THE BATTLE OF SARATOGA
ON OCTOBER 17.

1783
THE WAR OFFICIALLY
ENDS WITH THE SIGNING OF
THE TREATY OF PARIS.

1774
THE CONTINENTAL CONGRESS
MEETS FOR THE FIRST TIME.

1776
THE CONTINENTAL CONGRESS
ADOPTS THE DECLARATION OF
INDEPENDENCE ON JULY 4.

29

GLOSSARY

ally: one of two or more groups that work together

celebrate: to do special things for a holiday or other important day

confidence: belief in abilities

Continental Congress: the governing body for the colonies at the time of the American Revolution

defeat: to beat an enemy

document: a piece of writing

fortify: to make safer and more secure by building strong structures such as walls

inspire: to make someone believe something

myth: a story that is believed by many but is not true

patriot: one who supports their country

protest: a public show of disagreement

punish: to make someone suffer for a bad action

surrender: to agree to stop fighting

FOR MORE INFORMATION

BOOKS

Buckley, James, Jr. *Who Was Betsy Ross?* New York, NY: Grosset & Dunlap, 2014.

Keller, Susanna. *The True Story of Paul Revere's Ride.* New York, NY: PowerKids Press, 2013.

Ziff, John. *The American Revolution.* Philadelphia, PA: Mason Crest, 2016.

WEBSITES

Stories from the Revolution
www.nps.gov/revwar/about_the_revolution/revolutionary_stories.html
Read stories about different people and events of the American Revolution.

The Revere House
www.paulreverehouse.org
Learn more facts about Paul Revere's life.

INDEX